CW01316553

THAT AUTISM MOM'S

Guide to Homeschooling

That Autism Mom's
Guide to Homeschooling

By Shelli Allen

That Autism Mom's Guide to Homeschooling

Copyright©2016 by Shelli Allen. All rights reserved.

No part of this publication may be reproduced, stored in a retrieval system or transmitted in any way, by any means, electronic, mechanical, photocopy or otherwise without the prior permission of the author except as provided by USA copyright law.

The opinions and views expressed herein belong solely to the authors

It is not the intent of this document to dispense legal or medical advice. Nothing in this book should be construed in any way as medical or legal advice. All legal or medical questions should be referred to the appropriate professionals.

Published in the United States of America

ISBN-13: 978-1512360417

1. Disabilities / autism
2. Children With Disabilities / education
3. Homeschooling / General

Date: April 6, 2016

I dedicate this book to my incredibly amazing husband, Patrick Allen. He smiles and grins as I present him with every idea or adventure that I want to take our family on. He is supportive and generous to his family and deserves great honor as the man of our home. Homeschooling is a team effort, and I am so lucky to have him on our team. –Thank you Babe.

To my children, thank you for being you. You don't have to be famous or have a lot of money. You are perfect just as you are. You have taught me so much about life and how to dance in the rain.

Last, but never least, I give thanks to God. When I was weak, His strength was perfect. When I wasn't enough, He showed up and made the difference—every time.

A very special thank you to the leadership and families at Learning Adventures Special Needs Homeschool Academy for their loving support to our family.

Learning Adventures Academy

For more information about Learning Adventures
http://laacoop.blogspot.com/

That Autism Mom's Guide to Homeschooling

Table of Content

Introduction.................................pg. 11

History of Homeschooling................pg. 15

Benefits of Homeschooling...............pg.19

Different Styles of Homeschooling....pg. 31

Can I Legally Homeschool................pg. 37

Choosing Out-Side Services............pg.43

Don't Forget the Sensory Stuff..........pg.47

Daddy!! Daddy!!!..............................pg.51

Field Trips for Enrichment................pg.53

Field Trip Ideas...............................pg.59

Apps for Teaching..........................pg.62

Homeschooling Blogs I follow..........pg.65

A Letter from Me............................pg.69

Introduction

Before I had my children, and before I knew anything about autism, I wanted to homeschool. I was impressed by the families that I had met that were homeschooling. I saw families learning together, investigating, and enjoying one other's company. I was forming this "ideal" of what homeschooling looked like. From a distance all I could see was the 'picture perfectness' of mom, dad, and children walking along in perfect sunshine harmony.

While I was in public school, I always struggled to get the help I needed when I had a questions about what was being taught. I had my favorite subjects that I did much better in. School, in general, was not my favorite place to be. I was smart and had a small group of close friends, but other than that, I did my best to fade into the background.

I will always remember the High School chemistry teacher who started off the first day by telling us that if we were going to pass his class, we were going to need an outside tutor. He was the football coach. He was right; I didn't pass his class. I didn't respect him much as a teacher either. I'm not sure how a teacher can keep getting a paycheck without teaching his students anything. Maybe this is the moment that I began thinking about how great it would be to homeschool.

After marriage, my kids came along, and autism became a way of life for my husband and me. While I respect all the challenges that autism brings, my kids were presented with more than casual social challenges. I was in search of answers that would help me help my kids. My oldest, Josh didn't sleep. When I was pleading with our pediatrician for any kind of help, I got questions like, "Are you letting him nap during the day?" "NO!" I would firmly say. I had been asked this question more than once. I could see they clearly did not believe me that my son had really not slept for three days. It took a major event for them to introduce us to melatonin, and it has changed our lives with more sleeping nights than awake nights; for this we are so grateful. With each challenge, God provided us with exactly what we needed when we needed it. Homeschooling was one of those provisions.

I usually tell people that my kids were the poster kids for what to do if you receive a diagnosis of autism, before we started homeschooling. Both were diagnosed around the age of two. They both received extensive work ups from multiple professionals at the Thompson Center in Columbia, MO. Both started out in the early intervention program before they received an official diagnosis. Through early intervention we received the maximum hours allotted for ABA services along with speech therapy and occupational therapy. I had a therapist in my home every day of the week working with the kids. This was the greatest gift I could have received during this time in my life. I learned how to enter my kid's world and speak to them in a language that they would understand. I use what I learned during this extremely tough time in my life every day. I use what I learned to train churches how to work with kids with disabilities. I am forever grateful to those who played a part in this process. When the kids turned three, they graduated out of early intervention and into early childhood. They went into the public school special education program, and again we were met with amazing professionals who continued the process of teaching me new things while working beautifully with my children. They were my team. When Josh turned five years old, we had some decisions to make.

My husband had made a connection with one of his customers that helped us get the kids into a private school that had been on our wish list for a while. God showed up with provisions yet again. Both kids attended Rivendale Center for Autism a year and a half. It was near the end of this time that my heart started leaning back to homeschool. Maybe it was all the sleep I was getting. I was feeling 'super human' once again. This must have been God's way of preparing me for a life of homeschooling.

This book will be published before my homeschool journey is complete. Perhaps, I will write a part two. I have experienced so much already with homeschooling. The most important things I've learned are to:

1. Let go of the "picture perfect" homeschool ideals.
2. Let your children lead their learning process. No two persons are going to learn the same, so let them take the reins in their learning process.
3. Don't let stress run your days.
4. Don't let other homeschoolers (moms) tell you how to homeschool your kid.
5. Do your best to have fun. If you're having fun, they will too.
6. When it gets tough and you feel at your worst, take time to ask God for strength and wisdom. He has always come through for me.
7. Seize the moments!

--Shelli Allen, That Autism Mom

"Train up a child in the way he should go: and when he is old, he will not depart from it."
--Proverbs 22:6 (Homeschooling 1:1)

History of Homeschooling

"Homeschooling with autism is a journey. It looks like we are homeschooling and other days I imagine we look more like a zoo." –Shelli Allen

The modern homeschooling movement began in the 1970s when John Holt, an educational theorist and supporter of school reform, began arguing that formal schools' focus on rote learning created an oppressive classroom environment designed to make children compliant employees. Holt called for parents to liberate their children from formal education and instead, follow a method that today is known as unschooling.

Early Holt followers connected through Holt's newsletter, *Growing Without Schooling*, which was founded in 1977. Soon after, Holt's argument inspired the first homeschoolers. Holt's friend, educational theorist, Ray Moore, added his voice, arguing that early schooling was detrimental to children and that children should be schooled at home until the age of eight or nine in order to give them a firm educational, psychological and moral foundation. Moore's 1981 *Home Grown Kids* quickly became popular and was often the first book homeschoolers read.

> "What is most important and valuable about the home as a base for children's growth into the world is not that [it] is a better school than the schools, but that it isn't at all."
> --John Holt

When Holt and Moore first began advocating homeschooling, educating children at home was legal in all fifty states, but subject to varying regulations, which were sometimes quite stringent. Six states required parents to have a teaching license. Early homeschoolers generally worked with their local school boards, meeting requirements and submitting their home education plan. In the 1980s, Moore stated that in 80% to 90% of all cases, "local public schools are understanding."

During the 1980's, the tenor of homeschooling changed as a new wave of individuals entered the movement. These were evangelicals and fundamentalist Christians engaging in culture war rhetoric about public schools as "satanic hothouses" and were given credibility by Focus on the Family founder, James Dobson. Drawing initial support by Moore, these new homeschoolers took an agnostic outlook toward public school administrators and were unwilling to cooperate with the public schools they saw as evil. Many school officials felt threatened by the growing numbers of homeschoolers.

Moore and Halt's leadership did not last long past the 1980s. Holt died in 1985, and Moore was not respected by Christians to carry on the leadership. Michael Farris, a homeschool parent and attorney, became one of the new leaders of the movement. In the early years of the homeschooling movement, homeschoolers had generally worked together with the local public schools officials as was suggested by Holt and Moore. However, as relationships with local officials became more tendentious (because of the differences in beliefs by the evangelicals and fundamentalists homeschools), a variety of organizations, both religious and secular, engaged in legal efforts on behalf of homeschoolers and worked to change state laws. HSLDA was one of these organizations, though others did most of the heavy lifting while it was still in its infancy. In the early 1990s, HSLDA made a name for itself.

> *Meanwhile, homeschooling has continued to grow by leaps and bounds, especially as it has increasingly come to be seen as an acceptable educational alternative.*

Meanwhile, homeschooling has continued to grow by leaps and bounds, especially as it has increasingly come to be seen as an acceptable educational alternative. A growing number of families have begun homeschooling for neither pedagogical nor religious reasons, but rather for individual pragmatic reasons; including concerns with bullying, or the poor quality of local schools, and home education rates have increased more than 77% per year for the past few years. More and more colleges are admitting homeschool students. Great notice has been given to the usually better test results and graduations rates of homeschoolers.

Benefits of Homeschooling

"Homeschool Co-ops can be just the kind of support a family needs to keep up with the journey. Moms can chat about the ups and downs of the day and share ideas while our children practice social skills and build lifelong friendships."

An average of 2.53% of the school-aged population is homeschooled in each state. This number is growing each year. In the US alone, an estimated 1.5 million school-aged children are homeschooled. Many people are surprised to learn that homeschooled children scored higher than public school students on standardized tests. Homeschooled students scored 30-37% higher on standardized tests.
- Reading 85%
- Listening 85%
- Language 80%
- Math 82%
- Science 84%
- Social Studies 81%

SAT scores: Researcher, Clive Belfield analyzed data from 2001 SATs Belfield found that homeschoolers scored 80.5 points higher than public school whose average was 37.5.

Socially, homeschoolers have the advantage of participating in several activities in the community.
- 8% are active in Scouts.
- 10% participate in Ballet/dance class.
- 14% are involved with 4-H clubs.
- 25% are involved with other similar program.
- 33% perform some type of volunteer work.
- 34% are involved in some type of ministry.
- 35% participate in Bible clubs.
- 42% attend classes outside the home.
- 47% take music classes.
- 48% participate in group sports.
- 77% attend Sunday School.
- 84% go on Field Trips.

When I was contemplating homeschooling my children, I wanted to know if this was going to benefit them or hurt them. I looked at the pros and the cons. In my heart, I always wanted to homeschool, but after we found out that our children were diagnosed with Autism I didn't know if it was something that I could do. I definitely didn't want to homeschool if it was not going to benefit both of my kids. Many of my friends and family were concerned with my decision. Almost all of them, in fact.

Many people were concerned that it would be too exhausting for me. We all know that Autism never sleeps. This is definitely true in our home. If we did not have sleep medicine for Josh and Izzy, I would never, ever sleep. But we have found some great results in essential oils, melatonin supplements, and prescription meds. This gets us through most of our nights. My friends and family were worried that I wouldn't have "me time," but I didn't have much of that anyway. At first, I didn't know one homeschooling family that had children with Autism. I wondered if there was anyone with autistic children who did homeschooling. Well, after I started looking, I found a few here in my area that did. Two families to be exact. I was a little concerned, but something in my heart was driving me to keep looking into it. The internet was a great source of information for me. In general, homeschooling a child was very beneficial for many reasons, academically, environmentally, and socially. While most people, (those who don't homeschool) think that homeschooling a child is harmful socially, the research is showing otherwise.

I have found that people homeschool their children for different reasons. Here are a few:

Religious Reasons:
- Religious and family days can be planned and celebrated
- To develop morality
- To learn subjects that are not learned in school
- Work for internal satisfaction rather than external rewards

Family Reasons:
- Learn Family values
- Better education at home
- More time together at home
- Help out more with household chores and develop responsibility

Educational Reasons:
- Avoid crowded classrooms with too many distractions
- Avoid constant fear of embarrassment in front of teachers and peers
- Poor learning environment

Child reasons:
- Spend more time outside
- Protect from gangs, drugs, and guns
- Children with special needs can reach their full potential.

Looking at the Methodology of Homeschooling, I found many approaches. Many of them I could see working out great for my own kids. Most families were taking advantage of:

Community resources - such as museums, libraries, and Science centers geared to children.

Unschooling method - that nurtured a child's natural curiosity and provided learning within the moment.

Autonomous Learning - students get to choose what projects they tackle or interest they want to pursue

Online Education - which is educational programs online with online teacher support

Unite Studies - Parents use multiple subjects to teach their student one topic

All-in-one Curricula - Similar to conventional schools.

Student-paced learning - Students are allowed to progress at their own speed.

So what does this mean for those with special needs, and more specifically, for my children with Autism? Does homeschooling benefit them? Christopher J. Kicks, HSLDA senior counsel wrote an article called *Homeschooling a Struggling Learner* that was helpful to me. In his article he talked about, "teaching a child with special needs being a privilege-but also hard. It requires parents to sacrifice, to give unconditional love, and to consistently practice patience."

We have to realize that our children who have special needs experience struggles emotionally, physically and mentally. This is not easy for them as well. Our children's self-esteem is constantly being put into check. I am convinced that homeschooling my children, who have Autism, is the most effective way to successfully teach them. Our home is an ideal environment for them to learn, thrive, and achieve success.

As a parent, we often think, "How can I teach my child who has Autism? I have no formal training." Parents are doing it, and they are being successful at it. Objective studies show that parents are providing a superior form of education for their children with special needs by teaching them at home. In fact, in one of the most thorough studies on the subject, Dr. Steven Duvall conducted a year-long study involving eight elementary and two junior high students with learning disabilities. He compared a group of five students who received instruction at home with a group of five students who attended public schools. He was careful to match the public school students to the homeschooled students according to grade level, sex, IQ, and area of disability. Dr. Duvall sat in on teaching sessions and took an observation every 20 seconds, creating data points that were fed into a statistical analysis package. He had all of his work double-checked by a second observer.

Duvall recorded analyzed academically engaged time by students during instructional periods. He also administered standardized achievement tests to measure gains in reading, math, and written language. His results showed that homeschooled students with special needs were academically engaged about two-and-one-half times as often as public schooled students with special needs. He found that the children in the public school special education classrooms spent 74.9 percent of their time with no academic response, while children who were homeschooled only spent 40.7 percent of their time with no academic responses. He also found that homeschoolers have children and teachers sitting side by side or face to face 43 percent of the time, while public schools had this arrangement for children with special needs only 6 percent of the time. This showed a tremendous advantage for the children who were homeschooled.

In his studies, he further demonstrated that the students who were homeschool averaged a six-month gain in reading compared to only a half-month gain by the students in Special education in the public schools. Even beyond that his studies showed that homeschoolers also gained eight months in written language skills compared to their public schools counterparts. Dr. Duvall summarized, "These results clearly indicate that parents, even though they are not certified teachers, can create instructional environments at home that assist students with learning disabilities to improve academic skills. This study clearly shows that homeschooling is beneficial for students with special needs."[1]

With Autism being such a wide spectrum disorder, one size does not fit all. What works for one student doesn't always work for the next. I think as parents we have an advantage over teachers in the public school system for this very reason. So many great minds were homeschooled: Thomas Edison, Benjamin Franklin, John Wesley,

---

[1] www.hslda.org/strugglinglearner/sn_Klicka.asp

Beatrix Potter, Charles Dickens, and Alexander Graham Bell. Thomas Edison went to public school for three months, and they expelled him at age seven. The teacher thought that he was unable to think clearly and was confused. So many of our kids are also very misunderstood and thought to be unable to think and learn. This is clearly not the case for our kids; they simply just need to be taught differently. Parents who choose to homeschool know their children best. Who better to teach our children than us? It can be done, and it is an effective method of education. Edison himself stated, "She instilled in me the love of learning." Mrs. Edison overcame Thomas' disability, and he became a great inventor.

Another benefit to homeschool is the natural environment in which it is done. *There is no place like home.* This was a line from a song in 1822 by John Howard Payne. I happen to think that statement is so true. All children need to know that they are loved. To our children with special needs, this is even more important. Our children are aware of their differences, and this often leads to feelings of inadequacy. In homeschooling, parents can spend as much time as is needed to teach their special needs children how adequate they really are. We can spend extra time focusing on their strengths and incorporate those special interests in as much of their learning as possible. We can give our kids encouragement, no matter how small. If Josh uses his eating utensil for a bite of food, he gets a high five. If Izzy uses her words appropriately, there is another high five. We work hard, but we don't notice it as much with all the praise going on. My kids work even that much harder for me because I'm building their confidence with every praise and victory they receive from me. For more difficult lessons, we can approach from a variety of different angles to make sure the concepts are learned. We can devote as much time as needed to see that the information is learned without making our child feel slow or behind. Life applications are often the best teacher. Homeschooling provides the freedom to bring this approach to my kids' learning.

So many of my friends and family were concerned that homeschooling was going to be too much of a challenge for me. I was never going to get a break from my kids. 'Me time,' I think is what they called it. I didn't get to sleep much in the night because of the sleep challenges my kids had. I still wanted to homeschool. I wonder how many of them still think that I'm crazy for taking the leap. Let me tell you that after I have done this for a couple of years now, I have developed a new outlook for their concerns. While I do have less 'me time,' during the time I've been able to spend with my kids, I have found many benefits and personal fulfillment.

Let me give you a little background. My kids were in a great private school that specialized in Autism. All instruction was given with ABA methods. My kids were succeeding and doing well there. It was really a great school. I probably would still be there if personal circumstances hadn't pushed me further into my final decision to homeschool. When we finally settled into our homeschool life, maybe a month into it, I told my husband how liberated I felt. I felt such a peace about our decision. Both of my children started out in the early intervention program at two years old, and we had gone full force with therapies since then. We hadn't slowed down for almost four years. I wanted my kids back. I wanted to have a sense of normalcy in our lives. I could sense that with my kids as well. They were getting overwhelmed by it all. All the therapies, and going to and from school all the time. IEP meetings, evaluations, doctors' appointments, and therapy visits; our trips to the grocery store were the only times together that we could just be us. At home we had therapy bins set up, and we never stopped even after the therapist left. While I don't regret for one minute all the therapy and treatments that we did with our kids, I don't regret our decision to homeschool either. Early Intervention and the hours in therapy prepared me to teach my children. Coming home has been the best decision for our family. I integrate a lot of ABA concepts into our daily routines. Just because I'm homeschooling doesn't mean that all of their sensory problems and Autism challenges magically left. They are there, just not like they were before we started homeschooling.

Much needed flexibility

By being home in our natural environment, we are able to establish routines with the kids. We also have the flexibility of changing them if we need to. When the kids have had a terrible night or Josh has had a seizure, I don't have to stress to get them up and out the door for school in the morning. When we had to rush around to get to school, this was an added stress on the kids and made their productivity at school that much less. Behaviors were worse, and the meltdowns were intense. We have eliminated all of that. If there is an appointment during the day, I can plan the whole day around preparing for that appointment. This type of preparation makes our appointments much smoother and more effective. Flexibility is such a huge benefit for all of us.

I am more rested

One benefit that I didn't see coming, was that I am more rested. It didn't take me long to see this benefit. But the truth of the matter is that school doesn't last as long when you are homeschooled. Most days it only takes us about four hours to get through our daily lessons. We can break up those four hours throughout our day, however we see fit. I no longer feel rushed. Being rushed here and there is exhausting, and we don't have to rush anymore.

Sibling Friendship

We are always together. We go everywhere together. This was a concern prior to our commitment, but again I was pleasantly surprised by some of the observations I was making with my kids. They have become best friends. They still do a fair share of arguing, but they really are the best of friends. I think they understand each other and truly enjoy each other's company. I really couldn't be more proud to see this bond unfold. Not only is their bond with each other growing, but my bond with them is also growing as well. We are closer now as a family because of the hours we spend together each day through homeschooling. This type of bond is an important foundation for helping a family establish great values that will benefit them throughout their life. It is a sacrifice of my time, but completely worth it to me.

Time to prepare special diets

Many families who have children with Autism are on very specific diets like gluten-free or casein-free. It is a lot easier to monitor what your child is eating when you are the one feeding them. If eating good, clean food is important to you, then the way you eat is modeled every day. Your children will have a very good understanding about why this is important for them, without a lot of outside opposing influences. Most of all, that child will growing up knowing just how important eating healthy food is for his body.

I choose what is important to learn

There will always be the core subjects of Math, Reading, Science, Language Arts, History, Social Studies, Health, and PE. Within those subjects I can teach just about anything with my child's abilities in mind. I can also choose how I teach these subjects. My children always seem to learn better with manipulatives. They also show more interest when we include subjects or themes that they are interested in. For example, if your child likes cars, you can use cars as the theme for every one of those core subjects. Depending what grade level of math your student is in, you can count cars, sort cars, or create various patterns with the cars. You could pick a particular model of a car and find out all the history of that car and pick out specific historical events that were happening in the world during the time that the car was first manufactured. A trip to the library may be in order to gather information on a special interest car, and reading will be required. Spelling lists can be created from this same interest. See where I'm going? Getting your kids excited about learning is really important, especially early in life. A good basis for a joy of learning will create a lifelong learner. You will never go wrong by your child when this is accomplished.

The world becomes our classroom

I love it that I have the freedom to take our learning with us wherever we go. We are never confined to a table and chair. The more that we get out and explore, the more opportunities we encounter for discovering new interests for learning. The cycle never ends. Learning is always happening. I can go outdoors with the kids. Sometimes I miss this in the winter. My high energy boy loves the outdoors, and there is just something that is so soothing to him in this environment. This all goes back to the flexibility benefits as well. When we travel, we can take our learning with us also. Our kids can see up close and in person some of the great things we learn from our books. Students who are on the spectrum, are often times very literal. Seeing for them, is believing. This is a huge benefit for homeschoolers.

I have heard homeschooling referred to as "superior education." I have to say that I would to agree. Many children who are homeschooled tend to grow up with a more rounded sense of understanding about how the world works. Rebecca Kochenderfer, Senior Editor for Homeschool.com and co-author of <u>Homeschool Success,</u> talks about just how true this statement is in an article she wrote titled, *What About Socialization?* She wrote, "Socialization is actually meant to prepare children for the real world, which means learning to interact and deal with people of all ages, race, and backgrounds. In this case, homeschooling actually does a better job of this because homeschoolers spend more time out in society." In the classroom, kids are made to be quiet and not talk (socialize).

With the individualized time and care that a parent can put into their homeschool, students are given an opportunity to soar without restraint. They can learn about whatever they want, whenever they want with their parent guiding them to new levels of achievement each day. This is such a gratifying feeling for the parent and child. The possibilities are limitless.

Different Styles of Homeschooling

"Daddies are the best teachers and the most fun. I love to watch my husband get involved in the teaching process. It always looks like fun."
　　　　　--Shelli Allen

In my opinion, this is the least important chapter of this book. I only cover these details to help you decide what is best for you and your child. When you are starting out on your homeschool journey, you research all the options for homeschooling. Many families will choose a specific method of home education. There are a few types that I would like to share with you, and there very well may be more. The ones that I will cover are some of the more common ones. I will do my best to explain them to the best of my knowledge.

Schooling At Home
This is basically a set-up much like school. You would probably even have a classroom with desk and textbooks that were gone through much like you would at school. Many homeschoolers like to get away from this type of learning. It often takes away from the flexibility of special interest and levels of abilities.

Unschooling Method
This method is completely opposite of the previous method. I often see this method of schooling in the special needs community. Unschooling allows the student the liberty to choose activities as a primary source of learning. With this method, you teach in the moment. George Bernard said, "What we want to see is the child in pursuit of knowledge, not knowledge in pursuit of the child." The child is in control of their own education.

Montessori
Montessori education was developed by Dr. Maria Montessori as a child-centered educational approach based on scientific observations of children, birth to adulthood. Montessori puts an emphasis on independence, freedom within limits, and respect for a child's natural psychological, physical, and social development. Maria started out

teaching children in a mental institution. She was confident that this approach could make a great difference with appropriate techniques.[2]

Charlotte Mason
Charlotte Mason was a British educator who believed that education was about more than training for a job, passing an exam, or getting into the right college. She said education was an atmosphere, a discipline, and a life; it was about finding out who we were and how we fit into the world of human beings and into the universe God created. But this kind of thinking was pretty much eclipsed during the 20th century by demands for more exams and more workers.[3] Many homeschoolers have adapted this philosophy to fit their child's abilities. Many families find this approach to be very useful.

Online Homeschooling
We live in a technology-based world. Kids know how to navigate through programs and how to retrieve information from the computer with so much ease. Many parents find this type of homeschooling very beneficial. Many online sites offer a certified teacher to assist with lessons as well as record keeping for the parents. Parents may choose from a list of courses that their child will take, and everything is set up online. Many parents enjoy the convenience of this option. The specific needs of your child would determine exactly what option would be most appropriate for you. I like the convenience of lessons from apps that can be downloaded onto our iPhone or iPad. Many times these types of lessons are used in addition to other methods of learning. Many of our children with autism appreciate the predictability of a specific program.

---

[2] www.absorbentminds.com.uk
[3] www.amblesideonline.org

Classical Education
Classical education is based on the philosophy of education used in ancient Greece and in Europe during the Middle Ages. The philosophy of this style of education views education in three phases. These three styles reflect on a child's ability to reason. The first stage occurs when the student learns how to learn and has the ability to memorize many facts. The second stage occurs when connections are made of the facts that have already been learned. The third stage occurs when the student is able to articulate his own opinions. Many children will learn Latin when the Classical method of education is used.

Literature-Based Homeschooling
A couple of years ago, I attended my first homeschooling conference where I was introduced to Literature-Based Homeschooling. A representative from **Sonlight Homeschool curriculum** presented this method. It was my first time to hear of this approach. Rather than using textbooks, which can be uninteresting and bland to young learners, books are used as a curriculum. Students will be required to read or be read to from historical fictions and books written by people with a passion for their subject. This approach is designed to help your child develop a love for reading. With a love for reading a child's thirst for learning will never go dry.

Eclectic Learning
This method is the one that most homeschoolers will use. Parents will usually take components from several learning methods and put together an array of material with various methods intertwined. We use what works best for us. So should you. Find whatever works for you and just be confident in that.

There are other methods that I have not taken the time to discuss in this chapter. Over the years, I have found many free ideas and lessons on the internet. The public library is an excellent resource for families who choose to homeschool. Thousands of books are at your fingertips.

All of this information is nice to know, but not crucial. Many new homeschoolers often find this information overwhelming. I like to read over different styles and see if the method might be something that would work for my kids' learning style. I always like to say, "If you are not having fun, then your kids probably are not having fun either." Homeschooling is so much easier when everyone is having fun.

Can I Legally Homeschool

Homeschooling is now legal in all fifty states although requirements vary from state to state. It is always important that before you decide to homeschool, you check out what the laws are in your state. HSLDA is a great resource for finding out what your state requires of you as a homeschooler.

As your child's parent, you have a legal right to homeschool your child according to the first and fourteenth amendments of the constitution. If your child is currently in the school system and they have an IEP (Individual Educational Plan) that was set up by the school and special education team, you still have a legal right to homeschool your child. Sometimes we may feel intimidated by school officials and made to believe that we have fewer homeschooling rights than other homeschoolers because we are talking about individuals with special needs. Even though the constitution protects the rights of parents to homeschool, most state legislatures have passed statutes regarding homeschooling. This varies from state to state.

Hours of instruction by Missouri Laws

- 1,000 Hours of instructions
- 600 hours of the 1,000 above should be in Reading, Writing, Language Arts, Social Studies, and Science
- 400 of the above 600 hours are to be taught at home.

According to the HSLDA, Missouri laws are as stated:

Compulsory Attendance Ages: Between the ages of 7 and 17 years, or, at the parent's option, until the student completes 16 "statutory credits" (explained below) toward high school graduation. Missouri Annotated Statutes § 167.031. A student who has reached his 16th birthday is exempt from certain requirements (see below). § 167.031.2(3). If a five- or six-year-old is enrolled in public school, he becomes subject to compulsory attendance immediately until the parents request in writing that he be dropped from the school's rolls. Mo. Ann. Stat. § 167.031.1(3). Required Days of Instruction: 1,000 hours of instruction. At least 600 of these hours must be in the five core subjects below. At least 400 of the 600 must occur at "the regular home school location." Mo. Ann. Stat. § 167.031.2(2)(b). These requirements must be met within the school term (12 months or less) the parents establish. Not required for a student who has reached his sixteenth birthday. Required Subjects: Reading, math, social studies, language arts, and science. Mo. Ann. Stat. § 167.031.2(2)(b). These subject areas (including academic courses related to them) are not individually required, but must collectively constitute at least 600 hours of the child's instruction. Not required for a student who has reached his sixteenth birthday. Home School Statute: Mo. Ann. Stat. § 167.031.2.

Home School Statute: Mo. Ann. Stat. § 167.031.2. Home schools must meet the following additional requirements. 1. A home school is defined as a school that: a. "Has as its primary purpose the provision of private or religious-based instruction"; b. "Enrolls pupils between the ages of seven and sixteen years, of which no more than four are unrelated" (no limit on number of related students); and c. "Does not charge or receive tuition, fees or other remuneration." Mo. Ann. Stat. § 167.031.2(1)(a)-(c). 2. Home schools must maintain (but do not need to submit) the following records: a. A plan book, diary, or other record indicating subjects taught and activities engaged in (an appropriate daily log could satisfy this requirement); b. And "a portfolio of samples of child's academic work" or "other written credible evidence, etc."; c. And "a record of evaluations of the child's academic progress"; d. Or "other written, credible evidence equivalent to subparagraphs a) b) and c)" Mo. Ann. Stat. § 167.031.2(2)(a). Parents have the option to follow: a, b, and c, or they can choose to follow only d) which permits more flexibility. Missouri MO-2 Copyright 2014-2015, HSLDA, all rights reserved. May be reproduced only by permission. THIS ANALYSIS DOES NOT CONSTITUTE THE GIVING OF LEGAL ADVICE. Call or write to receive a free copy of HSLDA's newsletter and membership application. P.O. Box 3000 • Purcellville, VA 20134 • Phone: (540) 338-5600 • Fax: (540) 338-2733 • Website: www.hslda.org 3. When a child reaches his 16th birthday, he is exempt from all the requirements of paragraph 2, above, and also exempt from the requirement that he receive 1,000 hours of instruction. Mo. Ann. Stat. § 167.031.2(3). Between his 16th birthday and the automatic end of compulsory attendance on his 17th birthday, the only applicable requirement is that he be enrolled in a "program of academic instruction" that meets the requirements of paragraph 1, above. 4. "For the purpose of minimizing unnecessary investigations," parents "may provide to the recorder of deeds of the county where the child legally resides, or to the chief school officer of the public school district where the child legally resides, a signed, written declaration of enrollment stating their intent" to home school within thirty days after establishment of the home school and on Sept. 1 each year thereafter. Mo. Ann. Stat. § 167.042. Filing is strictly optional. Filing may compromise the family's privacy because the information is open to the public. Filing has occasionally caused a family to be investigated. 5. "Nothing in this section shall require a ... home school to include in its curriculum any concept, topic, or practice in conflict with the school's religious doctrines...." Mo. Ann. Stat. § 167.031.3. 6. Log defense. "The production by a parent of a daily log showing that a home school has a course of instruction which satisfies the requirements of this section [See 1 and 2 above] shall be a defense to any prosecution under this section and to any charge or action for educational neglect." Special St. Louis provision: production of a simple letter stating that the pupil is being homeschooled in compliance with the law is a defense if the pupil has reached his 16th birthday and lived in the city of St. Louis the previous year. Mo. Ann. Stat. § 167.031(5) 7. This statute was passed as a result of the federal court decision Ellis v. O'Hara, 612 F.Supp. 379 (D.C. Mo. 1985). The former law required home instruction to be "at least substantially equivalent" to instruction in the public schools. The court held: "This statute represents a prime example of legislation which yields an unacceptable amount of discretion to officials charged with enforcement. The statute, therefore, does not comply with due process requirements, and is unconstitutionally vague." Ellis at 381. The court applied "stringent scrutiny" because this case involved "the constitutional right of parents to direct the upbringing of their children and inculcate religious and educational values in their offspring." Id. 8. "Statutory credit." A provision in SB 291, effective August 28, 2009, created a new type of "credit." This new type of credit serves only one purpose: as a tool for giving families the option of exempting their child from compulsory attendance law before his 17th birthday. Since this new type of credit was created by statute, it is referred to as a "statutory credit." A statutory credit consists of 100 hours of instruction or more in a course that will count toward graduation. Homeschoolers are required to keep track of statutory credits only if they want to be eligible for exemption from compulsory attendance before the child's 17th birthday. Statutory credits are generally not used for preparing a transcript for submission to colleges, employers, etc. 9. "Home school education enforcement and records pursuant to this section [167.031], and sections 210.167 [compulsory attendance enforcement] and 211.031 [child in need of care] shall be subject to review only by the local prosecuting attorney." Mo. Ann. Stat. § 167.031.7 10. No municipal fire or police department, or state agency, department or political subdivision shall discriminate in employment based on the individual's elementary or high school education, so long as their program of education is permitted under Missouri law (which would include homeschooling). Missouri Statutes §105.255. Completion of a high-school level program of home schooling under chapter 167, Missouri Statutes, satisfies the initial education requirement for employment with the Missouri State Highway Patrol. Missouri Statutes §43.060.1[4]

Maintain the following:
- Plan book, diary, or written record indicating subjects taught and activities engaged in.
- a portfolio of samples of the children's work
- a record of evaluations of the children's progress
- other written, or credible evidence equivalent

---

[4] http://www.hslda.org/laws/analysis/missouri.pdf

Choosing Outside Services

"Our family has learned so much from therapist over the years. I take the information I have received from the great professionals and I use them in my kids learning process."

Some families worry about therapy needs when it comes to homeschooling. It is nice to have those resources if they are needed. I highly recommend sitting in on the sessions with your children so that you can carry on what is being taught in the therapy with your at-home learning. When working with children who have special needs, therapy can be highly beneficial. Cutting them out because you homeschool is not necessary. It also is not the end of the world if you chose to not add therapy to your homeschool schedule. Over the years, I have learned a great deal from our therapist. A lot of my teaching methods have come from watching and learning from the therapist and being directly involved with my kids' therapy sessions. We have taken breaks from therapy. I evaluate our need for them and add them in when something comes up that I feel unqualified to address.

Finding the right therapist is also very important. Finding professionals who understand how to work with autistic kids is sometimes a challenge. An initial interview with the therapist that does not involve the kids can be very beneficial. Then, bring in your children for an interview with the therapist and observe how the interaction goes. I think that a therapist who is willing to start off with pairing *techniques* prior to starting any treatment protocol is going to be a good therapist. If a connection is not established after a month or so, continue your search for a therapist that will be a good fit for your family. If you are with a therapist that does not support your choice to homeschool, then keep looking. That really goes for any professional who is involved with the care of your children. Remember, homeschooling is perfectly legal, and you are not doing anything wrong by homeschooling your child.

I like to say, "Homeschooling is not for wimps." Homeschooling with Autism is not at all for wimps. Having a support system in place is very beneficial for many reasons. Before I started homeschooling our kids, my husband along with others tried to tell me that I couldn't do it. They tried to tell me that it was going to be a lot of sacrifice and commitment. They all knew that it would be challenging to keep up with the daily needs and care of my two children who have autism. Some of our challenges that stem from Autism are sensory needs, communication needs (both of my kids are non-verbal), and our biggest challenge was sleep issues. When my kids were in private school, I would drop them off at school and come home and sleep while they were gone. I knew that just because my kids were at home with me, I wouldn't get my "nap" during the day. This was not only going to be the hardest thing I was going to do for my children, but I was also going to do it with little to no sleep. I must have sounded crazy to my husband and those who were encouraging me not to homeschool. My heart was telling me to do it. I thought I was tough enough to do this big thing all by myself with no help at all. I thought, "I'll just show them." For the most part I did. By the time the first doctor's appointment came around, I was looking for help. A couple of weeks without sleep, and I was looking for help. After our first winter, I was looking for someone other than my children to visit with. I got very lonely. After our first year of homeschooling was over, I was looking for ways to pull myself out of the burnout I was feeling.

I found a co-op that was amazing! I got the support of other moms who were homeschooling children with special needs. They planned regular field trips that were geared for our children. I was able to be involved with my children as much or as little as I needed. One of my favorite opportunities provided by our co-op is a time for mom Chats. The moms usually meet once a month for coffee and visiting. Getting together with these moms refreshes me and helps give me with new ideas. When I leave our 'little chats,' I feel ready to face another month of homeschooling. This has been a great support network for me.

Joining clubs can also provide an outlet. There are so many different special interest clubs to access for homeschool families. Sports can be used as PE hours. Champion athletes and the miracle league are a couple of clubs that are in the Springfield, MO area, and they cater to individuals with special needs.

Boy scouts and girl scouts is another form of activity and interaction that many homeschooling families take advantage of. If you are lucky to find a troop that is set up for children with special needs, this could be a great investment for your family. There are other clubs that are similar to boy scouts and girl scouts that may be worth investigating. Keepers of the Faith are like Girls and Boy scouts, but are more faith centered outlets. Keepers of the Faith allows you to create your own club. This way you can cater to your group's specific needs.

There are so many options available. It usually doesn't take long before you feel overwhelmed with all the choices. If you find one that you does not fit your needs or your child's interest, graciously excuse yourself from the particular group and continue your search. You are bound to find one that is perfect for your family.

Don't forget the Sensory Stuff

When we talk about required subjects to teach when homeschooling, we think of Reading, Math, Social Studies, Science, English, and Bible. When homeschooling with autism, adding in time to tend to sensory needs should be a must.

It is easy to get caught up in the homeschooling aspects and forget that your child may be needing sensory attention. Many children who are on the autism spectrum struggle with self-regulation. This is an ability to independently manage the sensory system. Sensory management can easily fall into a hierarchy of needs.

Several years ago, the public schools looked at children's hierarchy of needs as it related to a child's full learning potential. School lunches were already put into the daily school schedule, but now they were looking at providing breakfast for students before the school day began because many children were coming to school without being fed breakfast. Kids were tired and unfocused in their morning classes, making it more difficult to preform academically. The same instance can occur when our children are not able to effectively regulate. If any of the sensory system is out of balance, our children struggle with focus, behavior could be a problem, and learning could be the hardest task in front of your child. Take time throughout your learning to take sensory breaks. Everyone will be more willing participants when sensory needs are met.

I try and keep all of my sensory fidgets and gadgets easily accessible. Some lessons or activities pose as more of a focus challenge; especially for my boy. This is typical. Boys need to use those large muscle motor skills more often than our girls. I have found that more learning happens when I am literally actively teaching my son. For example, I encourage the use of sign language as a mode of communication. Josh understands signs very well, but has been super stubborn about using signs to request wants and needs. We have a large trampoline in our back yard. Josh loves to jump with me. I stop jumping until he signs for "more." If he wants me to stop, he has to sign "stop." We manage to get the sign "jump" only on the trampoline.

We also use big therapy balls. Therapy balls are great for wiggles while sitting and doing table work. We often add breaks where we cover the table in shaving cream. Shaving cream is calming for Josh, but not so calming for my daughter, Izzy. Some kiddos will be hyper-sensitive while others are hypo-sensitive. Knowing what your students' needs are will be key to managing a good sensory diet throughout your days. Sensory management should come before academics.

For my daughter, sensory breaks are a little different. Izzy needs large motor too, just not as much. Izzy needs deep pressure. She does a lot of her work in homemade tents and small spaces. This is how she works best.

Both kids love pillow fights. I love pillow fights too. Not only is this sensory perfect, but it is great therapy for the frustrations that build up through the day.

Nature walks are such a great release for sensory overloads. There is a lot of learning that can take place on nature walks. Safety lessons can be taught. How to stay on the sidewalks and how to watch out for cars works out great for teaching life skills. During the colder months when it is harder to get out and walk, we can take field trips to the Mall or grocery stores. The dollar store is a great place to learn shopping and money/budgeting skills in real life situations. Stores and indoor walking may need to be taken in smaller time frames.

Art time can give multiple opportunities to work the sensory system. Finger paints, painting with paint brushes, building bird houses, and much more can really help get through the core subjects. Kids learn best through play. So give your children free time to be kids and discover who they are. Give them the freedom to develop their own imagination.

Don't rule out cooking as a sensory activity. Baking cookies is such a motivating thing if the cookies are well cooked. So many lessons can be taught from the kitchen. Both of my children love helping out in the kitchen and are more advanced in the kitchen skills than most typical developing kids their age.

I try to involve my kids in every aspect of my daily life. This may include cleaning, cooking, and even laundry. One of Josh's jobs is to carry the laundry baskets to and from the dryer. This counts as a large motor input that Josh needs to get through his days successfully. My daughter loves to wash dishes mostly because she loves running water. Soap suds are Josh's favorite thing to play in. Another win for the sensory input!

Homeschooling provides so much flexibility to provide these natural environment training opportunities that teaches life skills as well as how to attend to his/her sensory needs independently.

Having a schedule in place can help with self-regulations. Having predictability in daily life helps build confidence and awareness which helps with other aspects of academic learning. Picture schedules paired with written words help to provide visual clarity and reading associations. Be consistent, but don't get so stuck in the routine that when hiccups happen in the schedule, meltdowns occur. Leave room for spontaneity; this will help them function in an adult world.

Daddy!! Daddy!!!

> "I love to watch my husband work with our kids. He always has the best ideas. He plays a key role in our success as homeschoolers. There is no way I do this on my own."

When I first told my husband my secret plan to homeschool our children, I believe he laughed at me in a smirkey kind of way. Like, "Ha yeah right. You won't and you couldn't" kind of response. That was in the beginning. I hear him now tell people with pride that his wife homeschools our kids. I think every mom I've talked to has said something similar about their husbands' response to the idea of homeschooling. No matter how hard homeschooling gets for us, we always pull through it and keep trucking along. We made a commitment to this because it is just that important for us.

I have heard of some Dads doing mechanics classes with the kids when they get a little older. Sitting down in the evening to read a good book to the kids is such a reinforcement to what mom is doing during the day. Dads have so much wisdom they can pass on to their children. The manner in which they do it is equally valuable. There is a sense of adventure when Dad gets involved.

My husband gives me the time I need to breathe. It get intense some days. The times that my husband leaves me at home and takes the kids for a couple hours is heaven on earth. It's hard to get caught up on housework and lesson preparation with the kids and their needs pulling at you. Someone said your house must be so quiet since your children are non-verbal. I laughed! My house is full of the craziest noises. The constant vocalizations that come from my kids' mouths are the things that sometimes grate on my last nerve. My husband helps me find my sanity when I feel like it has left me for good. The support husbands provide to the team deserves to be commended highly.

Field Trips for Enrichment

"Let your children's uniqueness shine through even out in public. My kids love to stop and play in water—even the mist fans at the zoo where we fit right in."

I love to take trips with my kids. It is always important to check out possible locations. Check for accessibility. I always check out the environment for possible stressors that my kids might face. When I know in advance what the environment is like, I can know what I need to do to help my children.

Websites will often have pictures posted of the area. Prior to going somewhere, we print out some of those pictures and put them in a "Social Story" book. This type of book helps our kids prepare for our trip and lowers their anxiety while the family is on the trip.

Field trips and vacations are such a great hands-on learning experience for homeschoolers. Many families take trips like these during the summer vacations. Homeschool families often take trips like these during the school year, when these locations are less busy and pricing is often cheaper. Going during a time that is less busy also provides some peace of mind for us autism parents, because it is a less stimulating environment with less people around. Whatever helps our children, makes for a more enjoyable trip for everybody.

Hands-on learning, where multiple sensory opportunities are available, is always the best learning method. See how field trips can enhance a child's learning? Being at the place where George Washington Carver lived, seeing where he did his experiments, and the type of tools he used to discover all those uses for a peanut, helps children's imaginations go wild. They start to get a sense of who and what we are talking about. These were real live people, and the things they did are not just an interesting story. I don't think you can get a better education than to experience these facts on a field trip with an educational purpose.

There are also other occasions for field trips that enhance a child's education. Hiking, fishing, swimming, and camping are all ways to speak to the "whole" child. So do not exclude these from your homeschooling schedule. In the Resources section of this book, take a look at some recommendations for possible field trips and adventures that your family can take as a part of your learning opportunities.

I can see the wheels turning in some of your heads. But my kids have Autism…taking my kids anywhere is an act of God. How can I even began to make any of this work with our family? So listen very carefully to me. I really want you to hear what I am saying. I too am that mom. I am 'That Autism Mom.' I still get anxiety when taking my kids to the grocery store. When we choose to homeschool our children, usually it is just us and our kiddos, **BY-OUR-SELVES**. A lot of times, we don't have a free hand to snatch and grab our kids from doing the embarrassing, unthinkable things. Keeping them from harm's way is also very real, especially when you don't have a free hand or an extra set of eyes. When we go out, there is no time for relaxing and enjoying the trip. We are on high alert. ALWAYS. Moms and Dads, hear me out. Don't let your anxiety keep you from doing things with your kids. Practice makes perfect. Start out small and work your way up to the big things and then **BREATHE**. Our kiddos need this life experience if they are going to be successful when you are not around. We have to give them opportunity to fail and to succeed. No matter what their cognitive development is, get them out of the house and give them real life experience. Letting our kids' find the things that they like and that they are drawn to, will later be their wings that help them soar through adulthood. It will help them with job

> *"The world is the true classroom, The most rewarding and important type of learning is through experience, seeing something with our own eyes."*
> *--Jack Hanna*

placement down the road. We have to start while they are young, by letting them explore the world that they live in.

Meltdowns are a part of our kids' communication tools. So look for teachable moments. Plan, plan, plan ahead. Take a couple of pieces of paper and fold them in half. This is the start of your social story. These do not have to be fancy or creative masterpieces. If you have to (I do this), on a separate piece of paper, write out each step that it takes to get through one task. Here is an example. Say we are going to the grocery store for a few groceries. Remember, small trips first! You want your children to experience success. This will build their confidence and reduce anxiety for them later on down the road. Here is my list.

Social story Check list:
1. Get your socks and shoes on so we can leave.
2. Go to the van (we have a van).
3. Drive to the grocery store (HyVee or Wal-Mart usually).
4. Get a cart (I instruct my kids to always hang on to the cart).
5. Go get milk, eggs, bread, and popsicles.
6. Go to the checkout (I always put a little reminder not to touch all the candy on the shelves in the checkout line. This is very difficult for my kiddos because they want it all.) Remember to keep your hands on the cart or help mom put groceries on the counter.
7. Go to the van. (I always put my kids in the van to keep them safe while I load the groceries into the van.)
8. Go back home.

Now with each one of these steps, I put a stick figure drawing of what is going to happen on each page along with a small description above or below the picture. Then, before I start asking the kids to put on their shoes, we read the social story. We read it a couple of times so that they can get in their head what is about to happen. Then, I'll maybe even read it again before we get out of the van to go into the store, to make sure that all those steps are fresh in their mind. Then we go for it. If by some chance we melt down in the store, I have been known to push my cart to the side and walk to a bathroom where it is quiet to let my kids regroup. Then I pull out my little story and try again or if a bathroom is not available, we go out to the van where I let them regroup and we try again, if possible.

> *"Homeschooled children have greater potential to work outside the box because they are educated outside the box."*

Sometimes, portions of the natural environment of grocery stores and shops include sensory triggers that affect my kids. Maybe it is a smell or the lighting that I cannot do anything about. This is where training becomes tricky. If the lights are what keeps setting my son off every time we come, then maybe we bring dark sunglasses. When they use the intercoms, the noise is too much, so we pull out head phones. There are times that I can distract my kids to where they are not even affected by the typical stressors. Sometimes, I'll pack little snacks that they really like. Yes, sometimes this is all it takes. If your children are still small enough to sit in the cart and play on an iPad while you shop, go for it. This too, exposes them to the environment. Enough exposure will help them build up a tolerance for the things that overload their sensory systems. I have seen a blog floating around Facebook about not letting your kids have iPads in church. Now get ready, I'm about to step up on my soap box for a brief moment. While I completely understand the basis for this article or whatever you want to call it (someone else's soap box), I am not against iPads in church, especially for our kiddos on the spectrum. They need time to desensitize from environments that are over-stimulating, and church is one of those places that so many of our children are not given this opportunity, because of stigmas that are formed through so-called, "good parenting practices." This is what training looks like. We have to give parents the room to do this with their children, without passing our own judgments off on them. Now I'm going to step off my so-called "soap box" and continue with my point. Take the time to train. No matter how many times you have to start over to see success, do it. I don't care if you have to put noise reduction headphones on and sunglasses to enter the store successfully; these experiences are exposing your kids to real life lessons. When they see that they can do grocery shopping and enjoy it without having a sensory overload, you can start adding items to your lists. Your trips will become longer, and you will eventually have a complete and successful trip. This my friend, is what homeschooling is all about. This is why it is a success. All of your "field trips" can be learning opportunities just like this, but you have to first be willing to start out small.

Field Trip Ideas

"Grandparents are such a nice addition to the Homeschooling process."

Possible Field Trip Ideas

Lewis and Clark Boathouse and Nature Center
@ Bishop's Landing
1050 Riverside Dr.
St. Charles, Mo 63301
Ph: (636)947-3199

Katy Trail State Park
302 First Street
Boonville, MO 65233
Ph: (800) 334-6946

Mark Twain Museum
3735 Shrine Road
Florida, MO 65283
Ph: (573) 565-3440

Precious Moments Chapel
4321 S. Chapel Road
Carthage, MO 64836
Ph: (800)543-7975
Email: chapel@preciousmoments.com

Harry S. Truman Museum
Independence and Grandview, MO
223 N. Main St.
Independence, MO 64050
Ph: (816)254-9929
*Tours are $5.00 charge. Self-guided tours are FREE

Jefferson National Expansion Memorial
11North 4th Street
St. Louis, MO 63102
Ph: (877)982-1410
Web: www.nps.gov/jeff/index.htm

Fantastic Caverns
4872 N. Route 125
Springfield, MO 65803
Ph: (417)833-2010
Web: info@Fantasticcaverns.com

Silver Dollar City
330 Silver Dollar City Parkway
Branson, MO 65616
Ph: (800) 475-930
http://www.silverdollarcity.com/theme-park

Magic House
St. Louis, MO
516 S. Kirkwood Road
St. Louis, MO 63122
PH: (314) 822-8900
Web: www.magichouse.org

Autism Apps: *some educational and some not so much

- Choice Works
- Pro Lo Quo
- My Play home
- Sensational brain
- Wait timer special needs app: www.friendshipcircle.org/apps
- Smart Apps for kids
- Smart Apps for special needs
- Math Bingo
- Teach Me Series
- Alpha Tots
- Tally Tots
- Letter School
- Glow draw
- Star Fall ABC's
- Islands
- Hungry Fish
- Hooked on Phonics
- ABC phonics
- Khan Academy
- Bible for kids
- Bad piggies
- Sort it out
- Montessori Apps
- Science 360
- Let's learn how to draw
- Scribble Press
- ABC Magnetics Board
- Sacciarelli
- Splash Math

- Native Numbers by Native brain
- Letter school
- Classify it
- Alligator Apps
- Grandpa's and Grandma's apps
- Grandpa's tool box
- Grandma's Kitchen
- Toca Boca Apps
- Play Lab Apps
- Gozoa math
- Todo Math
- Todo time
- Rocket Speller
- Toca Nature
- Toca Kitchen
- Toca Town
- Toca Lab
- Monument Valley
- Math Mystery Town
- Montessori Math
- Slice fractions
- Toontastic
- Ansel and Clair
- Homer
- Sago Sago
- The Human Body by Tiny Bop
- Windowsill
- Stack the States

*Recommended for Low functioning Children and or Toddler Apps

- Heat Sense
- Finger Works
- Squiggles
- Egg Roll Apps
- Owlie Boo
- Sprinkle Jr
- Petting Zoo
- Build it up
- Dots 4 tots
- Little writer

*This list was compiled by members of Learning Adventures Co-op **moms: Michel** Smith, Jessica Adams, Tisha Chambers, Elizabeth Wiley Exley, and Ellen Kuentzel

Homeschool Blogs I follow

- **Homeschool Sanity**
  https://www.facebook.com/motivatedhomeschooler

- **SHEM Homeschool Ministry**
  https://www.facebook.com/SHEMHomeschool

- **Practical Homeschooling**
  https://www.facebook.com/PracticalHomeschooling
  Website: http://www.practicalhomeschooling.com

- **Special needs homeschooling**
  https://www.facebook.com/specialneedshomeschooling
  Website: http://specialneedshomeschooling.com

- **Homeschooling**
  https://www.facebook.com/pages/Homeschooling

- **Homeschooling Ideas**
  https://www.facebook.com/Homeschoolingideas

- **Bible Based Homeschooling**
  https://www.facebook.com/BibleBasedHomeschooling
  Website: http://biblebasedhomeschooling.com

- **HSLD**

https://www.facebook.com/hslda
Website: http://www.hslda.org

- **Heidi St. John, The Busy Mom**
  https://www.facebook.com/heidistjohn
  Website: http://heidistjohn.com

- **Todd Wilson, The Familyman**
  https://www.facebook.com/ToddWilsonFamilyman
  Website: http://familymanweb.com/

You can find me at the following

Living the Life As My Kids Mom
http://livingproverbs31asmykidsmom.blogspot.com

Website: https://www.thatautismmom.com

Find me on Facebook:
https://www.facebook.com/thatautismmom1

Find me on Twitter @thatautismmom

A letter from me:

Hey there! I know that making the decision to homeschool is a scary one. Not everyone is cut out for it. If you're not, there is no shame in admitting it. Know that I have days when I feel like I'm not cut out for homeschooling. My kids go through developmental growth spurts that throw us for a loop. I cry...just being honest. I made a decision to homeschool, and some would say they are "called" to homeschooling. I believe I was. As my kid's mom, I wanted to gift them with a home education. I wanted to homeschool before I had kids. I liked the idea. When we received the diagnosis of autism in both kids, I thought my vision of homeschooling went out the window along with typical parenting. My heart and gut said, "Why not homeschool?" As I looked into homeschooling and saw what kinds of benefits it had on kiddos with special needs, I was ready to take the "homeschool leap." Homeschooling is a way of life. I look for opportunities to include my kids in everything I do. I almost always have to make adaptations, but I am an autism mom. It is what we do. We make PEC's card and social stories to bridge gaps for communication. We advocate and speak up for the needs of our kids. By including my kids in my everyday life, I am training them to function in "real" life. Our education is not situational. Public school kids that are on the spectrum or even those with other special needs get to the end of their school life and begin 'life skills.' My kids started with life skills, and I find this benefits many later on in life. I believe in home education. It is a commitment much like a marriage. I don't always love it, but I am committed to seeing it through. I know that I will have successful days that are roses and butterflies and other days that quite literally feel like hell on earth. I don't say this to scare you, but to give you real life perspective. As you get started, I want you to remember this... Your first year of homeschool will feel like the honeymoon. You will spend the most money your first year. A lot of moms do their best to recreate "public school" their first year. They will buy marker boards, complete sets of curriculum, and fancy desks and chairs. In the second year, you take what didn't work the first year and you try new stuff with less zeal; you then really start to question, "Should I be homeschooling? I'm not sure I'm cut out for this." The second year is the hardest, I think. The third year usually provides the most realistic look at how you will homeschool your kids for the long haul. By that time, you will have developed a really good idea about what you will use and what kind of outside supports you will need. My last piece of advice strongly encourages you to find a group of homeschooling moms who are on the same special needs journey as you and have coffee with each other once a month. This has been golden for me.

This is all I have for now. I wish you well on the exciting journey.

--Shelli Allen, that autism mom